DADDYHOOD

DADDYHOOD
THIS CHANGES EVERYTHING!

DANIEL W. DRISCOLL

SORIN BOOKS   Notre Dame, IN

© 2002 by Daniel W. Driscoll

www.sorinbooks.com

International Standard Book Number: 1-893732-42-8

Cover/interior illustrations by Dan Slattery

Cover and text design by Brian C. Conley

Printed and bound in the United States of America.

Library of Congress Cataloging-in-Publication Data
Driscoll, Daniel W.
Daddyhood : this changes everything! / Daniel W. Driscoll.
      p. cm.
ISBN 1-893732-42-8
      1. Fatherhood. 2. Father and child. 3. Father and child--
Religious aspects. I. Title.
      HQ756 .D68 2002
      306.874'2--dc21
                                                      2001004615
                                                              CIP

FOR FELICIA

Grow old along with me!
The best is yet to be,
The last of life, for which the first was made:
Our times are in His hand
Who saith "A whole I planned,
Youth shows but half; trust God: see all, nor be afraid!"
—ROBERT BROWNING

Contents

Acknowledgments

This book is the result of input over the years from many friends and family members. I am truly grateful.

As a good Irish boy—and out of fear of retaliation—I will first acknowledge my parents, Pat and Norm. They seemed to thrive in the midst of the frenzied world of parenthood. My earliest childhood memories are of laughter and delight.

Friends have revealed to me the many-faceted character of love and have shown me that "family" extends beyond bloodlines. My memories of Kyra Loudermilk have not faded in the twenty years since her death, though the world remains duller without her. Patricia Hackett's friendship is truly a friendship in the eternal—the love existed long before we met. She and Michael Horan have been my constant companions for many years, and my strongest supporters. My students in New York—many of whom became friends—told me to keep telling stories. Pat and Ken Capolino and their family gave me a home away from home. Meals, conversation, and laughter in their house kept me grounded. Graduate school classmates helped me to wrestle with questions of life, God, family, and relationships.

Michael, Ellen, Mary Beth, and Anne Marie grew up with me and taught me how to have fun in the midst of childhood's chaos. Charlie, Carole, Jane, and Dave joined us and taught us how to be family in a new way.

Most importantly, I am grateful for my wife, Felicia Leon-Driscoll, who let me out of the house to write about the goings-on inside the house. Every word I have ever written passed by her loving and insightful eyes before anyone else could see or hear it. She is my creative source and my purpose.

And of course, my thanks go to the ones who turned me into a daddy: Padraig, Clare, Jack, and Liam. Since the day they emerged from the embrace of their mother's womb, they have invited me to experience a hope-filled abandon that I would never have known without them. A loving, merciful, compassionate (and playful!) God dances on this earth through them.

Introduction

Life is no brief candle to me.
It is a sort of splendid torch
which I have got a hold of for a moment,
and I want to make it burn as brightly as possible
before handing it on to future generations.

—GEORGE BERNARD SHAW

I have noticed since becoming a father that it is difficult to sit on the floor. No longer can I lean my head against my hand, elbow on the floor, popcorn in a bowl to one side of me, watching something on TV. This has nothing to do with physical conditions of thirty-somethinghood. Rather, the problem is that I am fair game as soon as my torso drops below the imaginary line that separates the serenity of grownup space from the wilds of kidspace. I go to the floor and four children jump me, try to find whatever piece of flesh has not yet been attacked by a sibling, and then implant a knee firmly into that flesh. I tried counting once to see if there

11

were really only eight knees among them, but they were too fast for me—I couldn't get an accurate count.

"Any man can be a father," reads a magnet on my brother's refrigerator, "but it takes someone special to be a daddy." I suppose that is simplistic sentiment, but there is a truth to it. Daddy receives the knees in the stomach, yet later returns to the floor, undaunted. Daddy climbs into a warm bed, knowing that he will walk the hallways at least once before the sun comes up. Daddy sometimes wonders why he got himself into all this, but wakes up after a night of interruptions ready to try it all again.

I have spent five years as a daddy, and I have laughed and cried and pleaded my way through them. Fourteen months after our first son (Paddy) was born, Felicia and I welcomed our daughter, Clare. Sixteen months later, Jack was born, and before the eldest even turned four, our fourth child, Liam, was born. Unconventional as it might be today, Felicia and I chose to do it this way. We desired a big family with children close in age, and God did not disappoint. We are still undecided as to whether God is merciful or a comedian. Perhaps God is both.

Becoming a dad changes everything. This book addresses that change. It attempts to discover some serenity in the midst of living with small children, a life that at times seems far from serene. It offers an opportunity to reflect on the present moment—rather than waiting until the children grow older—to make some sense of it all. It attempts to be deliberate in parenting, deliberate in prayer, and deliberate in finding a virtue in fatherhood even in the most chaotic moments.

There is no real order to the stories, chronologically or otherwise, since so often there seems to be no real order to this life. They are not meant to be read at one sitting; rather they are meant to be read occasionally, over time. Each ends with a prayer as a hope that in the midst of living this life, we might direct some of our attention to that which is bigger than us.

Some of the stories will ring true to the reader's experience, some will not, but my hope is that underlying the stories is an experience of "daddyhood" that strikes a somewhat universal chord. Life to a three-year-old can be, among many other things, an experience of wonder and delight. These reflections aim to uncover some of that wonder and delight, and in so doing, even welcome the chaos. Quiet, better-ordered days will come, and as appealing as those days are, I do not want to miss today's wonder.

The reflections in this book are by no means written by an expert. They are written by a daddy and a husband who seeks to find meaning in this new life as a father. Often this is not easy to do, but at night, when it is quiet and the children are asleep, sometimes God's clarifying grace penetrates the darkness. These reflections celebrate that grace.

CHAPTER 1

Brownies and Minestrone

Trust yourself.
You know more than you think you do.

—DR. BENJAMIN SPOCK

The birth of our first child was a combination of excitement and delight, worry and concern, brownies and minestrone.

Felicia and I had spent nine weeks in a childbirth preparation class, and one of the tips we had received was to bake brownies for the nurses at the hospital to get them on our good side. Felicia went into labor on a Sunday morning. Since the contractions were still relatively gentle and far apart, we went to church, took a long walk around the lakes at the University of Notre Dame, and then went home. Felicia left to finish up at her office in anticipation of her maternity leave, and I went to work in the kitchen, baking the prerequisite brownies.

At that time I was a full-time graduate student who loved cooking. I had prepared many meals for the freezer for the early weeks after the baby was born, and one of those meals was homemade minestrone soup, something my wife claimed to enjoy. I decided to warm up some of that frozen soup for Felicia's return from work, for a light meal before labor got intense.

Proud of myself, feeling very clever for having prepared this meal ahead of time, I warmed the soup and took the brownies out of the oven. Little did I know what my combining the smells of chocolate, tomatoes, and green peppers would do to the woman who was about to become the mother of my child.

Felicia arrived home, took one breath, and said with a disdain I had not experienced before, "What is that *awful* smell?" Opening all the windows, turning on fans, I quietly responded, "dinner." Oops.

Looking back on that first experience of labor, I can see that it was in many ways a symbol of our relationship. As much as Felicia and I try, we cannot always guess what the other is thinking, or how the other will react to something we say or do. As far as parenting goes, each of us has an individual style, and presumes the other understands it. We couldn't have known this before the baby was born.

One of us thinks it is perfectly acceptable to offer the kids a snack at 3:30 in the afternoon, and then wonders why they don't eat dinner; the other would have them eat bread and water for breakfast and nothing else until supper, just to assure a peaceful dining experience. One of us would keep the television in the closet; the other lines up Sesame Street videos alphabetically for Saturday afternoon enjoyment. One of us thinks the combination of brownies and minestrone is not an unusual smell; the other suggests that it is an especially cruel form of torture for a woman in labor.

Embarking on the journey of parenting, this new phase of our love, we longed for new life, we longed for something more, we longed for God. Our souls thirsted for this, and we were eager to begin. It required courage, but instead I think God blessed us with ignorance. If we had known what was to follow, perhaps all the courage in the world would not have been enough.

God of our hearts, we long for you,

for your peace and your strength.

Be with us in the mystery of childbirth.

Remain with us on the journey of parenthood.

Protect our love for each other

and for the children you have brought us.

Grant us your wisdom and your mercy.

CHAPTER 2

A Question and an Answer

When Samuel went to sleep in his place,
the Lord came and revealed his presence,
calling out as before,
"Samuel, Samuel!" Samuel answered,
"Speak, for your servant is listening."

—1 SAMUEL 3:9B-10, NAB

I have been out of touch with Jim for a while. He and I had once relied on each other for friendship and support. He was unmarried and had no children. We would often joke about the grass being greener across the other's fence. Jim longed for a day when he would have children, and I longed for a day when I could go to a movie whenever I wanted. He liked hearing stories about my kids, and I liked hearing about his weekends away. He thought the discipline of caring for small children was admirable, and I thought his freedom to train for a marathon was enviable. He put a hot tub in his backyard; I shopped for a swing set.

Jim remembered our kids at Christmas, and I think the gifts he gave them were a part of his longing for something more. I knew that longing, since when I thought about his life of relative independence, I too longed for something more, something different.

The friendship faded once he met his true love. He no longer had time to hear about sleepless nights, chickenpox, and amusement park kiddy rides. He was now involved in a life of excitement and romance. I remember talking to him one Thursday afternoon. He was in a hurry to leave because Thursdays boasted a special happy hour. "Oh yeah," I thought, "happy hour. I remember that concept." He would snowboard on a whim and buy a new bike because he wanted it. His was a life that I too had once lived, but by now had practically forgotten. His life was a whirlwind of adult activity; mine was still defined by diapers and Disney. Jim's romance brought him a newfound interest in life, and I found myself missing the days when he thought that diapers and Disney seemed exciting.

The grass was now greener only on his side of the fence. In fact, he wasn't even looking over at my side anymore. He no longer envied me for my lifestyle, but as much as I tried not to, I still envied him.

The experience of Jim's friendship caused me to look at my life in a way I hadn't before. Everything I had ever hoped for had come true—I had married the woman I loved and we brought four children into this love. Now, however, I saw some flaws, and I felt tired. There was little time to talk to Felicia because of the children's demands. When we did talk, it was most often about them. The sleepless nights seemed longer, and I was less patient with the children's behavior during the day. Some of the fun of being a daddy was slipping away.

Perhaps it was a natural human tendency to ask what might have been had I made different choices. Perhaps it was normal to wish for a little more freedom, a little more independence, and a little less responsibility. Perhaps it was natural and normal, but nevertheless I didn't like it. I needed to be reminded of what I had right in front of me. I needed an opportunity to remember the gift that I had been given. My daughter's middle-of-the-night tears soon gave me such an opportunity.

A call from Clare's bedroom brought me to experience the God who set the stars in their place, caused the earth to bring forth life, and brought this little child into our world. Crying, Clare couldn't tell me what she needed. I went through the usual list—her doll, a cup of water, her blankets pulled up differently, the door opened or closed, a song, a trip to the potty—but nothing was right. She couldn't tell me what she wanted or needed. She just cried. Finally I said, "Clare, do you want me to come into bed with you?" Nodding her head, she pulled the blankets down for me.

I climbed into her twin bed, maneuvered my way among the books and stuffed animals, and managed to get under the sheets. Clare turned to me, smiled, placed her hand on my chest, her head in the crook of my arm, and immediately fell into a deep sleep.

All was quiet. Felicia and Liam were asleep in our bed, Paddy and Jack were asleep in their room, the stars were set in their course, the heavens and the earth were lined up as they should be, and Clare was breathing deeply. A peace came over me at that moment, a sense of communion, an undeniable presence of God who had pursued me in love from the beginning of time, and whose love was now embodied in the people who slept in my house.

I did not need a weekend away; I did not need a happy hour; I did not need to go snowboarding. I needed to curl up with my baby and be enveloped in the love that formed me and continues to make me the person I am.

I will always remember Jim, not only for the friendship we shared but for the way he allowed me (albeit unknowingly) to re-connect with the family I love. Insight comes unexpectedly, often from surprising sources. Jim's presence in my life created a question. Clare's call to me that night answered it with absolute clarity. The question was about the worthiness of my life and the wisdom of choices I had made. The answer was faithfulness. That night I was Samuel, hearing the voice of God calling me into the sanctuary. It was not until I allowed myself to say, "Speak, Lord, for your servant is listening," that I truly recognized the voice.

God of faithfulness, I hear your call,
and I turn to you in my questioning.
Reveal your presence to me
in the daily life I have chosen.
Help me to see that it is you
who guide me to peace.

CHAPTER 3

Watching the Night

If I have seen farther than others,
it is because I was standing
on the shoulders of giants.

—ALBERT EINSTEIN

D ad was Big Dipper; I was Little Dipper. Today, my more liberal tendencies would probably object to the whole thing entirely, but thirty years ago I was in heaven, sitting on someone's living room floor, wearing a feather on my head, surrounded by other boys with feathers on their heads, making unnecessary beaded things. My father was sitting next to me, also wearing a feather. This was the YMCA Indian Guides, and my dad and I were a team.

In so many ways that scene feels like it belongs to someone else's memory. But I believe there is even photographic evidence somewhere to prove it. Today, finally a dad myself, I smile at the thought of his coming home from the office, taking off his suit, and donning a feather to go and sit in someone's living room to watch his kid burn the words "Little Dipper" onto a leather medallion.

My father, however, thrived on that kind of thing. He was a master at the art of daddy-hood. Childhood for us was filled with wonder. Footprints of soot trailed from the fireplace every Christmas morning; Mary Poppins was often seen in the city during the workday (reported back to us at dinner-time); the football in the backyard was snapped to the sound of a fruit or vegetable ("banana, apple, celery, CARROTS! Hike!"); and bad jokes kept us smiling ("What does a dog say when he sits on sandpaper? 'Rough! Rough!'"). He loved his kids, he loved his friends, and he loved my mom.

I often think of him now that I am trying to do what he did back then. I often wonder if it was an effort for him, or if it all came naturally. When I read to my kids at night, I try to remember if he read to me. When I throw kids into the air while standing chest high in someone's pool, I think of what it was like for him to throw me in the air. I remember fondly a certain way he had of flipping us over his head while he lay on his back on the floor, but I can't for the life of me figure out how he did it. When all four kids are demanding my attention at once, or none will sleep, or they fight with one another, I wonder what it was like for him. Did it just come naturally?

I think of how obvious it was to us that he was crazy about my mom, and I wonder how I can make that obvious to my kids too. I think about the way he treated everyone with dignity and respect, whether they were bank executives or they were cleaning the floors and running the elevators. I wonder if my kids will see that in me. I think of how he gathered friends around him and created a home of laughter, games, and song. I wonder what my kids will remember.

My children have developed a custom on summer nights. After baths and all the nighttime rituals are complete, they often ask if they can go out on the porch with me and watch the night. This the easiest, most pleasant time of the day. The kids sit in their chairs and I sit in mine, looking for stars. When the stars start appearing, they begin announcing each one they see, along with the "star light, star bright" rhyme. They seem disinterested in the fact that the rhyme is about the FIRST star they see that night, because they repeat it and repeat it many times, over many stars, before they are done. Sometimes they announce their wish; other times it remains a secret. I think the announced wishes are the ones that they most desire, recognizing that it might be advantageous for them that I hear such wishes. But always they take this time of the day to just stare at a deep blue sky and let their conversation flow through fantasy, dreams, jokes, wishes, and fears. It is often the most real time we spend together.

I love watching the night. What my kids don't know is that one of the reasons I love it is that while they are seeking their stars, I look for one particular constellation. One constellation, with its telltale pattern of four stars in a box and three stars shooting up from one corner, looks down upon my daddying. One constellation always approves of me, even though I often fall short, do things wrong, make bad decisions, lose my temper, and fail. One constellation looks back at me, and somehow I feel like it is saying that yes, indeed, fatherhood suits me, that fatherhood is good. I am a grown man looking at that constellation now, sitting next to my small children, but I still look at it as the person I will always know myself to be, the Little Dipper.

I will never know if fathering came easy to my dad. My kids, though, sit next to someone who experienced the wonder of his stupid magic tricks. My dad has never seen me father anyone, since he died when I was in college, but watching the night with my children somehow brings us together. It connects my kids to their past, and, since my father's blood pumps through their hearts, it connects him to the future as well. Those nights of sitting in rocking chairs and spouting off wishes somehow bring my kids face to face with the Big Dipper himself, complete with feather and leather medallion around his neck.

No, fathering does not always come easily or naturally. But I try to hold on to what is most important, to what attaches me to my past. Then I too can make a home of love and laughter, and I too can bring wonder into my children's lives.

God of my upbringing,
hold those who went before me
closely in your love.
Let a spark of my own childhood
keep warm the embers of my children's.
Let any hard memories
serve to deepen, soften, and protect the time
spent with my children today.

CHAPTER 4

The Deepening of a Love

*The most important thing a father can do for his
children is love their mother.*

—FR. THEODORE HESBURGH

We have a wall of pictures in our family room.
Eight-by-ten portraits of our six-month-old children hang as constant reminders of their baby-
hood. There are some pictures from an Easter several
years ago: little children with bunnies. There is a poem
written by a friend for our wedding day, framed forever
as a promise. In the midst of these pictures and words is
an eight-by-ten portrait of two people with smiles that
won't quit. One is wearing a white gown, a family heir-
loom. The other, beardless and beaming, wears a tuxedo
and white tie. Sometimes I find myself staring at that
photograph, trying to remember who those two people
were. Was that picture taken only eight years ago?

Sometimes the most difficult aspect of becoming a
dad is remaining a husband, a partner, a friend, a

confidant, and a lover to the woman who shares this life with me. Daddyhood frequently can seem to take precedence over partnerhood. At the same time, I often wonder who she is. Is she the children's mother? Is she her parents' daughter? Is she my wife?

Of course she is all of these, but still none of these facets defines her. She is a person of depth and intelligence that knows no limits. She is a profoundly open person, a woman constantly becoming. Yet all too often, because of the pace of our lives, I see her only as the one on the floor separating the blue blocks from the red ones.

Becoming a couple is an ongoing journey into the undiscovered. When the gown is put into storage and the tux is returned to the rental shop, the work of living begins in a new way. Living takes a sharp turn when the pregnancy test is positive, and then plummets into the unknown when the baby's head emerges. Discovering each other and rediscovering each other in the midst of parenting is a lifelong challenge.

I have left our bed countless times because the third occupant—a squirming baby—kicks me out. When I turn on my way out of the room, I see that Felicia is still sound asleep, peaceful in that kicking company. I have handed babies to her when they are not quieting down, and have witnessed their instantaneous expressions of peace in her arms. I have tried to tell stories to her, only to be interrupted so many times in the process that I forgot what the story was. Amazingly, I usually discover that she had kept track the entire time. I have watched her read books, assist with crayons, nurse, and do the laundry all at once. I have seen her pour out her love on our children, and I have wondered if there will ever be a day when I feel like her offer of love is not a choice between them and me. I am embarrassed that I think this way—*of course* it is not a choice between the two—

so I wonder when I will return to acting like her partner, and not someone more childish than her own children. However, that is easier said than done.

Sometimes it feels like the marriage is on hold while we focus on changing diapers. It feels like we have entered a type of twilight zone, a buffer between the days of being a couple and the days of being, well, a couple again. I look forward to the day when I can stand next to Felicia at church again, since right now we either go alone, or go with the whole family and then chase kids throughout the service. I hope that day will happen before we are standing at the wedding of one of our children. It feels like the last time it happened was at our own.

There is no solution to all of this other than forcing ourselves to make time for the other. We have to make dates, even if the date is a cup of tea on a Tuesday evening after the kids have gone to bed, letting the laundry and the kitchen go, and just being with each other. Clare and Jack both are very good at asking me to hold them—Felicia and I should follow their example.

We need to take friends up on their offers for an afternoon of babysitting. We need to show each other that we remember that the other is more than someone's mommy or daddy. We need to do many things. Admittedly we don't do any of it enough—the laundry and the kitchen can wait, but we cannot.

Music has a way of bringing the past into the present. Playing the song that we danced to at our wedding places me back in that reception hall and brings Felicia back into my arms. All the hope and idealism celebrated on our wedding day is still a part of our lives, but we need to be a bit more deliberate in accessing it. Hope and idealism, along with romantic love, are not in themselves the natural partners of potty training.

I love these days of chaos, but I don't want to turn to my wife in fifteen years and say to her, "Now tell me about yourself." I need to be saying that to her every single day, so that the time will not come when I have forgotten who she is, and the woman in the photograph becomes just someone I used to know.

God of all promises,
help me to remember the woman I married,
and forgive me for the times when I fall short.
May I hold her tightly
in the midst of the turmoil.
Keep my heart ever connected to hers.

CHAPTER 5

Suppertime

The soul is healed by being with children.

—FEODOR DOSTOYEVSKY

"**P**addy, sit down, please." "Clare, take your hand out of your cup." "Honey, catch Jack. He's standing up in his highchair again." "Yes, I will butter your bread, Clare, but how do you ask nicely?" "Paddy, when you are seated we will start." "There goes Jack again. Honey, could you grab him? Maybe he needs his cup." "Hey kids, we don't talk so loudly at the table." "I hear Liam. Where is he, anyway?" "Clare, I love that song. Could you sing it a little more softly?" "Let me put the cat out. He's about to jump on the counter." "I'll nurse Liam, you take the peas off the stove." "OK, Paddy, you can tell me your joke now." "I don't see any whole milk—do I give the kids the two percent?" "No, Clare, we drink milk or water at dinner, not juice. You know that." "Paddy, please sit down. OK, go to the potty, and then we will start." "Can you grab a cracker for Jack? He's standing up again." "Did you wash your hands?" "Paddy's back. Now let's say grace."

We had friends over the other night for dinner. I am sure they thought that they had taken a wrong turn and ended up in a scene from *The Little Rascals*. By the time we said grace, their eyes were like saucers. That moment of peace—when hands are held around the table, thanking God for all we have been given—is often the only moment when all of us are actually focused on the same thing at the same time.

Felicia and I rarely sit down at dinner for more than a few seconds, and never at the same time. I am sure that buzzers on our chairs go off as soon as we sit. The buzzers either awaken Liam, remind Paddy that he needs more milk, tell Jack to pound his plate against the wall, let Clare know that it is time for the potty, or any number of modifications on the theme.

Suppertime is for sharing, certainly. I ask the kids to tell me about their day, and—when I resort to questions that require a yes or no response—I sometimes get the information I seek. That does not mean they do not talk, of course. They talk constantly about whatever they choose to talk about. Answering their dad's questions is not always a priority. Their priority is usually for a different kind of conversation: "You're a bumble bee!" "I'm not a bumble bee, but you're a turtle!" "Don't call me a turtle! Mommy, Paddy called me a turtle!"

Jack is often naked by the end of the meal because it is easier for us to take off his clothes in the highchair than it is to clean the wallpaper on the staircase leading to the bath. Somehow, if he is still wearing his clothes, the wallpaper will contain bits of mashed potatoes, carrots, and the remnant of whatever else we ate for supper. We have the suppertime highchair/high wire act figured out, so that at the precise moment when he has stood in his highchair for more than thirty percent of the meal, we start his naked ride up the stairs to the tub.

Suppertime is an athletic event, worthy of a spot in the summer Olympics. The challenge is to remember in the midst of it that these children are the same children who give unsolicited hugs, who sit on my lap for long stretches of time reading books, who always remember to remind us about goodnight kisses, who love to explore flower gardens, and who love to paint with watercolors. They are the work of God's creative genius, the same creative genius that gave us thorns on roses, days of rain followed by days of brilliant colors, and the caterpillar to whom we sacrifice some garden plants so that one day we will see a butterfly. God is in the thorn, in the rainstorm, in the caterpillar, and in the suppertime frenzy.

The prayer we offer at the outset of the meal is not separate from the experience of the meal itself. True, the kids are quieter as we address God, and the handholding keeps their attention, but God is also addressed in the whole experience. God, whose love created both the peace and the frenzy, is present when Clare is called a turtle, when Jack stands in his highchair, when Liam awakens at the least opportune moment, and when Paddy tells a joke.

We do not merely tolerate the thorn for the sake of the rose, but we love them both, as they are equally of God, formed in love to glorify their creator. The child who disrupts dinner is the same one who peacefully curls up on my lap. We love both, and in so doing we celebrate the child's abundant, multicolored, ongoing praise of God.

God who loves both the roaring seashore
and the still pond,
may I praise you in the noise and in the quiet.
Remind me to love the thorn as I love the rose,
and in the midst of the frenzy,
remind me of the tranquility.

CHAPTER 6

"But Daddy Said I Could"

I don't know why I did it,
I don't know why I enjoyed it,
And I don't know why I'll do it again.

—BART SIMPSON

For my comfort level, Paddy began his "I'm-going-to-take-advantage-of-every-opportunity" stage far too early in life. Before he even turned four, he had figured out how to play one parent against the other. It is in the very genetic makeup of the human—the fine art of getting one's way—so it shouldn't surprise me that it begins at so early an age. While our particular experience only involved a *Peanuts* video, I know full well that around the corner is the inescapable Saturday night when Paddy takes the family car, leaving each parent convinced that the other gave approval for the joy ride.

I had been up relatively early with Paddy. We ate breakfast, talked about the day ahead, read a book, and fought about the video. The house rule is that—with few exceptions—rented videos are watched after supper, after baths, in the dark of night. While the sun is out, there are far too many things to do to allow videos to rule the day. He knows this, of course, but he also knows that the above-mentioned exceptions involve short videos—less than an hour in length—that we occasionally let the kids watch during the day. Given this loophole, he tried his best to convince me of the harsh injustice of the general rule and the contrasting generosity and fairness of the exception. Felicia had rented not one but two videos the night before, so there was a yet-unwatched video calling out to him from the family room. If there were ever a day for the exception to be implemented, this was the day. I, however, was not moved by his argument.

Clare and Jack soon woke up, and I set up breakfast for them. Paddy's lament seemed to ease, so when Felicia came downstairs with Liam, I thought it was safe for me to take my shower and get ready for work. When I came downstairs for the series of "good-bye, have a good day" kisses, I heard an odd sound emanating from the family room. It sounded like that teacher from the Charlie Brown specials that I had watched as a kid. I hadn't heard that sound in years, so I knew it must have been some mistake. It couldn't be coming from my family room.

It wasn't a mistake. A glance into the room revealed that my victorious son was smiling at the antics of Snoopy, Woodstock, Peppermint Patty, and Charlie Brown. Felicia said, "It is only a half-hour show, so I thought it would be OK this morning." The other three children were being a handful, so this was an innocent enough strategy on her part to be able to complete her morning tasks. "That's fine," I said, "but I spent the morning telling him why he could not watch that video."

The TV was turned off faster than Lucy could have pulled the football away from a charging Charlie Brown. "Don't you ever ask Mommy for something that Daddy already said 'No' to," Felicia said in her best serious voice. I'm not sure whether Paddy's tears were for the loss of the show he believed he was entitled to or for being caught implementing his creative diplomacy. Either way, I think we all learned something that morning. We all learned that we have a very long road ahead of us.

I hide the car keys now, in preparation for Paddy's inevitable Saturday night attempt to play one parent against the other. After all, it is only twelve years away.

God who leads us, help us act as one,

supporting each other in our parenting,

so that our children reap the rewards.

Let love be our bond, and love be our guide.

Let love be our discipline.

CHAPTER 7

Fragrant Sword Fights

Children have neither past nor future . . .
they rejoice in the present.

—LA BRUYÈRE

I will admit I never was much of a flower guy. I wasn't the kind of boyfriend, fiancé, or husband who frequented the florist, surprising my beloved with the colorful, aromatic harbingers of "I love you." However, in the old days—pre-kids—when the time came to break down and buy flowers, at least I was pretty sure that they would go into a vase, sit on a table, and look nice for a while. I was confident that they wouldn't be used as fly-swatters.

Today, however, anything is likely. I surprised Felicia with flowers not long ago and was soon impressed by the sheer creativity displayed by my children in response to having flowers in the house. My son used them as science experiments, putting food coloring into different glasses of water and watching the colors change in the petals. My daughter kept carrying two or three around the house, clipping them at the buds, placing the buds on tables and bookshelves here and there. The long flowerless stems remained, a vision of the old Addams Family series that Clare will someday think was produced around the time of Abraham Lincoln. Jack ended up using these spare stems as batons, swords, and brooms. When it became less fun to use just the stems for this, he started taking more flowers, sharing them with Clare, and having wonderful, colorful, aromatic sword fights with her.

Within twenty-four hours the happy little surprise for Felicia was spread all over the house, needing to be tracked down (it is amazing how many places flower stems hide, and how easily flower petals slip into difficult-to-reach places), swept up, and hauled out. The science experiment was only somewhat successful, and the fencing partners still proudly displayed their green hands. The one flower that remained looked beautiful in its own bud vase—way up high on top of the china cabinet—a certain glow radiating from its every surviving pore.

Flowers, I now understand, belong to children. They are no longer allowed to be messengers of sentiment alone. They are soft and fall apart nicely. They can be thrown and batted and dragged. They smell pretty and look good tucked behind one ear. They look much better in a doll's house than they do on the kitchen table. They can be stuck between the screen door and the front door to greet any guest that might stop by. Flowers help bugs move faster when they brush up against them on the patio outside. Cats deserve flowers by their litter boxes, and the refrigerator, you must admit, is much more palatable when a flower is masking-taped to its door.

We quickly learned to appreciate that one flower remaining in the bud vase, as if it were a simple reminder of a former life. Yet the one surviving flower, more importantly, reminded us of the regenerating power of laughter. The spontaneity involved in surprising one's spouse with flowers is rewarded with a smile. The children's response to such an event, however, is squeals and laughter. The former is satisfying, but the latter is downright healing.

The eleven flowers that sacrificed themselves to the joys of childhood are themselves, in many ways, this new life of parenthood. Our very identity has changed. Life is messier and less organized. We are spread thin, and find bits of ourselves scattered in many places. Sometimes it is even painful, or we are forced to be somewhere we would rather not be.

Yet we also fly through the air with joyful abandon, and are used by our Creator for things that we never dreamed we could carry out. We are bruised and wilted, perhaps not as beautiful as when we were on display in the shop, but we are in the business of forming humans who can love life. We are doing what we were created to do. We were finally taken off the shelf and put into the hands of children.

Let that one flower remain in the bud vase, because it is, indeed, beautiful. However, I will keep buying all twelve.

God who pushes forward, help us to look back
and see the days of our courtship and early marriage.
Remind us of the alone times,
the days of heart-stopping, stomach-churning new love.
And then return us to the present, renewed,
to rejoice again in the offspring of that love.

CHAPTER 8

Ice Cream Pilgrimages

*Blessed indeed is the man who hears many gentle
voices call him father!*

—LYDIA M. CHILD

Felicia and I spell I-C-E-C-R-E-A-M so fast that you would think we are saying our own names. We even have shorthand for it: "Hey honey, wanna go out for some I-C-E-C?" We attempt to communicate with each other—like all parents have attempted to communicate since the beginning of parenthood itself—without disclosing the entire message to little observers. Occasionally this backfires, because at times the children assume the worst about whatever we are spelling. My comment the other day, "Clare seems to be T-I-R-E-D" was met with Clare's insisting, "No I'm NOT!" I don't know if she understood the spelling or if—unlike her father—she was simply practicing full disclosure, loud and clear. She will not be talked about, no matter what is being said.

However, for the most part, the spelling works. "Ice cream" became easy to spell because we use it so often. Summer evenings are often spent with a combination of ice cream cones and goats, since Kerber's Dairy offers not only the homemade frozen confection, but also a farm, complete with farm animals. Our kids love it. For a dime, they can get a handful of feed that the goats lick right off their hands. Ten dimes later, their hands are licked so clean they are perfect for holding ice cream cones.

Elderly women sit at picnic tables, eating their ice cream. Felicia and I sit with them and watch the children from their vantage point. There is a lot of room for running at Kerber's, and our children take full advantage of it. The women's faces brighten as our children approach, and their conversation changes from neighborhood gossip to stories about faraway grandchildren.

These ice cream pilgrimages continue into the fall. Boasting hayrides and pumpkins, Kerber's meets our autumnal requirements. The staff creates a maze by cutting paths in fields of dried corn—a fun concept until our two-year-old gets confused and decides to ignore the paths and barrel through wherever possible. We often choose pumpkin-flavored ice cream at that time of the year, and the goats and llamas are still eager to lick our children's hands.

The day might have been crazy, the kids might have been wild, but there is a peace to Kerber's that settles us. Kerber's is a respite, a place where we can relax after dinner and enjoy each other. It is a place with a time and order of its own, a chance to sit on a bench, look at our children through the eyes of a stranger, and fall in love with them again. Ice cream pilgrimages bring us to a type of sanctuary where the simple elements of sugar cones, goats, and other kids' grandmothers momentarily protect us from the harder elements of life.

In earlier years, I would have gone to a monastery for a retreat. Now I go on retreat whenever Felicia says, "Hey honey, wanna go out for some I-C-E-C?"

God of rest and re-creation,
keep us united in the quiet times.
Lead us to refreshment
and teach us to love the simple gifts you offer us.

CHAPTER 9

She Found Her Soul Today

Pray without ceasing.

—1 THESSALONIANS 5:17

Sometimes it is 8:00 p.m. or so when I realize that the conversation that Clare began when I got home at 5:00 is still going on. Often at her bedtime I realize that I have heard the same voice continuously for three full hours. Occasionally I can alter the flow by escaping into the bathroom, but often that doesn't even work. The conversation continues from the other side of the door.

The conversation does not require the vocalizations of two people. Rather, the second person is required simply for presence. I do not have to speak, but once in a while I am allowed to nod my head or say, "That's wonderful, Clare," or something along those lines. Coincidentally, these conversations often fall on a day when her nap just didn't happen. The pitch increases until Clare's final, dramatic collapse at bedtime.

Many times I listen closely but can figure out the scene she describes only after I look to Felicia for a translation. "Applesauce?" I say to Felicia, "What happened with the applesauce?" Discovering that the kids helped Mommy make applesauce that day, I can continue with the conversation. Sometimes, though, tossing the phrase to Felicia results in a shrug even from her, the person who witnessed Clare's entire day. We just don't know where she got the story about the alligator, the leprechaun, and her doll.

Sometimes Paddy is my translator. "What was that, Clare, you found your soul today?" "No, Daddy, she found her soul. Soul. Soul. You know, like a snail lives in." Oh, I understand . . . shell. "Yeah, that's what I said. She found her shell today."

One night in the midst of one of Clare's conversations, I remembered the Thessalonians passage, "Pray without ceasing." That, I believe, is what Clare is doing during these (let's be honest and call them what they are) monologues. It is ceaseless prayer, words from a child about the gleeful state of childhood, a child glorying in the mystery of life and reveling in the wonder of the moment. Clare's words are about the beauty of the colorful socks she is wearing, the bunny rabbit she saw in the backyard earlier in the day, the surprise visit of one of Mommy's friends that morning, and even the nice pants I am wearing, but her words are really about more than all that. Clare is taking in every miracle that the day brought to her doorstep.

Someday these words will be formalized into the prayer that we will teach her. For now, her life is her prayer, and our Christian tradition honors that. Joy and wonder, frustration and lamentation, anger and rejoicing—it is all found in our tradition, in the praise and lament of the psalms, in the stories given to us by the generations who wandered in the desert, and in the words of the earliest Christians. Clare's desire to relate her day to her dad—to share in the very experience of living, to honor the moment—is all a part of the ancient prayer tradition into which she was born.

All of us were born to glorify God. The birds do it by being birds, the mountains do it by being mountains, and Clare does it by being Clare. Her words are telling me that a spider sneaked into the family room that morning, but her words are nonetheless a prayer to the God who created the spider, who listens to her every word, and who puts scripture quotes into my head to help me make it to bedtime.

―――――――――

God of patience, hear my prayer.
Bring me to the wonder of the moment,
and help me to join my children in ceaseless prayer,
so that in my words and in my living
I may glorify you, your creation,
and your abundant love.

CHAPTER 10

Putting Down Roots

There are only two lasting bequests
we can hope to give our children.
One of these is roots, the other wings.

—HODDING CARTER

S ome people would say it was a good problem to have. I was asked to interview for two jobs at the same time. One was a promising career in a big city. I would walk into a building each morning where I would be welcomed by the words "International Headquarters" emblazoned in brass letters above the door. My position would cover a nationwide region, and I would be traveling a great deal, including overseas travel. I interviewed, was offered the position, and took my family to visit the city and look at houses in the suburbs. I loved the opportunity and the people with whom

I would be working. Energetic and committed, they were a great group.

The other position was in a smaller city. As it turned out, though both interviews were scheduled around the same time, I was offered the first job before I interviewed for the second. I did not respond to that first offer because I wanted to interview in good faith. I was intrigued by the second position and wanted to give it a chance, but Felicia and I were convinced we had already made up our minds.

The second position was in South Bend, Indiana. I had attended graduate school at Notre Dame, and Felicia had earned two degrees from there. We knew the place well—the community, the schools, the people, and the churches. We had fond memories of that area where we spent the first three years of our marriage. Our first two children were born in South Bend. I would give the interview a shot, but as much as we liked the community, and as interesting as the job seemed to be, the first position was to be our choice. I would work in a big city, live in the suburbs, and travel to exotic destinations. I couldn't imagine anything more exciting.

As it turned out, however, something more exciting was around the corner. The morning I was to fly to the interview in South Bend, Felicia took a pregnancy test. Number four was about eight months away.

Suddenly the idea of international travel was no longer so interesting. Living in a suburb and commuting had lost its appeal. Bringing a pregnant wife with three small children to a place where we knew nobody seemed impossible. My priorities re-examined, I was now truly open and ready for the interview at the second job opportunity.

In a world where nothing seems to remain the same for more than a few hours, Felicia and I decided to commit to stability. In South Bend I am able to be home every single night. Never do I have to leave my family for weekend work, and the travel is very limited. Work is a seven-minute drive from my doorstep. No brass letters above the door announce it to be the entrance to an international headquarters, but I eat lunch with my children almost every afternoon.

The generations that came before Felicia and me took this stability for granted. Our families were grounded in their communities. Grandmothers were just a few front porches away. Aunts and uncles were available for Sunday dinner, and cousins knew each other's favorite colors, along with each other's secrets. Neighbors waited for babies to grow so they could watch them play baseball on their high school team, watch them leave the house on the way to a prom, and watch them try to sneak back into the house after their curfew (telling the kids' parents all about it the next day, of course). The butcher knew to stock up before one family's big Fourth of July cookout, and he remembered to save soup bones for another family. My children's great-grandparents were rooted in the depths of community, a community they relied upon in hard times.

Felicia and I realized early in our marriage that we would most likely never live down the street from our siblings, and our children would not play on the same teams as their cousins. Community, nevertheless, remains an important dimension of our lives. Digging in and nurturing roots is our job now. The international travel will come later.

We miss being around the people who lived in the houses in which we grew up, but now our kids run to the fence yelling "Ben! Ben!" every time our ninety-year-old neighbor walks out of his garage. Our neighbors noticed the activity at the house surrounding Liam's birth, and they all stopped by to welcome him and to check on Felicia. They stop our kids from running into the street, and they keep an eye on things when we leave for vacation. Our church sent meals to us after Liam was born, and they celebrated his baptism with us—the same people who celebrated the baptism of our first-born. Connections we made with people here during our first year of marriage are sustaining us in our eighth.

Our children will most likely dig up these roots someday, but in a world that values money and things over people and relationships, we want our children to know that their parents tried to ground them in the latter. We hope that when they set their own roots down—in whatever ground is right for them—they might remember running to see Ben next door, and they might remember that the people around them cared about their recitals, their teams, their proms, and their curfews. And if they never have a recital, play on a team, or attend a prom, we hope they know that the people around them cared about who they truly were, not only about what they did or what they accomplished.

Most important, perhaps, the people around them care enough to tell their parents when the kids sneak in after curfew. It is only fair. My mom's neighbors did it to me.

God of wisdom,
be with me in the midst of the difficult decisions,
keep my priorities always before me:
the wholeness, health, and happiness of my family.
Direct me in ways to be faithful to them.

CHAPTER 11

Dancing Into the
Emergency Room

*Let them praise God's name in festive dance,
make music with tambourine and lyre.*

—PSALM 149:3

I t was to be an easy task. I volunteered to have a hand-ful of eighth graders over to the house for a two-hour class. I had done it before. I had been a high school teacher for a number of years. I could handle writing a lesson plan and was confident in my ability to be with these kids for one evening. What I had neglected to remember, of course, was that all of my previous experience had occurred prior to the birth of the children who were supposed to remain upstairs while the class was in session in the living room. As it turned out, it was not such an easy task. Then again, nothing is really easy anymore.

The students were to arrive at 7:00 p.m. My wife had our kids in the tub while I made last-minute preparations downstairs. Just before the doorbell announced the arrival of the first student, I heard a piercing scream from upstairs. Piercing screams are no longer unusual in our house, so I continued my work. I didn't take notice until I heard Felicia's "Dan, get up here!"

Clare had been dancing in our bedroom while Felicia dried her brothers after their baths. Apparently the pure ecstasy of the moment moved Clare to try a new dance routine. The full twist and leap that would have made Ginger Rogers proud ended with the back of Clare's head landing on the corner of our dresser.

Running upstairs, all I could see was blood—on the carpet, on my wife, on the bathroom sink and floor, and all over Clare. Still, Felicia and I were certain that she would be fine. Head wounds, we remembered, always create a lot of blood, so not to worry. The bleeding would stop, the students would arrive, the cookies and milk would be eaten, and all would be fine. The bleeding, however, did not stop.

The first student to arrive was Logan. His father, who is a friend, went upstairs to check on things while I tried to organize the rest of the arrivals. Coming downstairs, he announced that he and Felicia were taking Clare to the hospital, dropping the boys at his house on the way. Himself a parent who had experienced many trips to the ER, we trusted his decision to go. Felicia and I would have talked ourselves into believing that the cut was OK, only to set the stage for Clare's later work on a therapist's couch. "They left me to bleed," I could imagine her saying, "all because Daddy had a class to teach."

Three stitches later, Clare triumphantly returned to the scene of the crime, more interested in the doll that the nurses gave her than the injury that had occurred several hours earlier. The next day we telephoned all the aunts and uncles and the grandmas in order for Clare to report on her adventure. My mother, who parented five children (born within a six-year stretch), had only one thing to say to me, and I think she believed it to be a comfort: "Get used to it. You'll know the ER like your own family room soon enough."

Murphy's Law states that anything that can go wrong will go wrong, and being a father of small children, I have learned to respect that law. Yet despite the injury, Clare had delighted in the dancing and in her new doll. She was happy to retell the story and to receive the appropriate attention. With nothing more than an unusual new haircut as evidence, her pain and fear faded into the bliss that childhood can be. Anything that can go wrong will go wrong, but with Clare, that which went wrong just as quickly became that which delights.

Any possibility for order that night was lost in the power of the music that impelled her to dance. Yet the class did take place, the stitches did heal, and the hair did grow back. What is most important is that Clare's wonderful full twist can still make Ginger Rogers (and the angels) proud. There may be a lack of order, there may be a risk, but we rejoice in the fact that the dance continues.

*G*od who creates and sustains all that exists,
enter this life in all its disarray.
Show us your peace in the midst of uncertainty,
and comfort us in the midst of pain.

CHAPTER 12

Plastic Snowmen and Broken Dishes

C is for Cookie, it's good enough for me;
Oh cookie cookie cookie starts with C.

—COOKIE MONSTER

S omeone mentioned a new Kenny Rogers CD to my
wife recently, and she perked up. "Mr. Rogers has a
new CD?" she exclaimed with joy. Realizing her
mistake, she laughed at the slip-up, but then confided
that she was actually disappointed that it wasn't Mr.
Rogers. She could have used a new CD by the beloved
man in a cardigan.

Our tastes have changed since becoming parents. At
Christmastime last year, I shopped for a tacky plastic
lighted snowman and was drawn in by the glamour of
the plastic Santas, elves, reindeer, and even the plastic
nativity scenes. I argued with the manager at Wal-Mart

because I couldn't find a huge, spinning, glowing, Ho-Ho-Ho-ing Santa and his sleigh for my rooftop. What kind of Christmas would it be without a display to light up the whole street? Our days of tiny white lights, candles in the windows, and crystal angels—teetering on table edges—are long gone. We are living in the midst of plastic now.

When I was a twenty-four-year-old teacher, I was amazed that I already did not know the music my students were listening to, and they were a mere six years younger than I was. Today, it is much worse. If the song does not involve counting ducks, I don't know it. If the kids are in the car, Raffi is king. If they are not, I don't turn on the radio for love of the quiet.

Turning on the TV to watch the news is strictly forbidden, since "mommy and daddy shows" are never permitted before bedtime. We can watch those boring shows when our kids are asleep, but during the hours of the day when they are walking, talking, and tormenting, only larger-than-life, multicolored animals are allowed to grace our screen. It's OK, however, because I have grown to prefer those shows to the news anyway.

The spot on the right shoulder of almost every shirt I wear is no longer an embarrassment but a badge of honor. My baby spit up on that shoulder this morning, thank you very much. I used to change the shirt before I left for work, but now that we are on our fourth child, that level of vanity seems uncalled for.

Scanning the ads in the Sunday paper—on those rare weekends when the paper is actually opened before it hits the recycling bin—no longer involves looking for porch furniture, tools, ties, or lawn mowers. It now is a frenetic search for highchairs, diapers, children's videos, and Noah's Ark wallpaper. Great deals on hedge trimmers and bottles of single malt scotch go unnoticed and the clothing sections of department store ads are not even glanced at, unless of course the ads have footy pajamas in them.

The four little lives that we brought into this world now rule it. Visits to friends' houses reveal just how much our tastes have changed. "Did you see that Waterford bowl they had out on that coffee table? Anyone could just pick that up and throw it against the fireplace. Who would put something like that out where people have access to it? How tacky." "Decorating" for us now means moving the breakables six inches higher with every growth spurt.

Crystal and china break, wallpaper rips, and new carpet stains. Many of our wedding gifts were not even removed from boxes after this last move. Our end tables and coffee tables are bare except for the occasional stray truck or Lincoln Log, and candles are no longer lit for atmosphere; they are purely utilitarian now. If "Happy Birthday" is not being sung, candles remain in the drawers unless there is a power outage.

Yet the broken items can be replaced, an interior decorator can be invited to visit us later, and Christmas can be a Victorian masterpiece once again. Someday the stereo will play our music again, the wedding gifts will be used and displayed, and a white carpet will remain white. Someday the children will roll their eyes because their parents are not cool enough to know their music, and Noah's Ark wallpaper will not even be a suggestion for their room.

Right now, however, we can all celebrate the music, the snowmen, and Mr. Rogers. We are in this together, so the rest can wait. Our tastes will change back someday, but today we are too busy marking walls with little lines denoting children's height. In the future that might look tacky, but today it is a Rembrandt.

God who never changes,
be with us in the midst
of our constant changing.
Keep our eyes set on the present,
dwelling neither on the past nor the future.
Help us to love what the day brings.

CHAPTER 13

Visiting a Foreign Culture

*The ornament of a house is the friends who
frequent it. There is no event greater in life than
the appearance of new persons about our hearth,
except it be the progress of the character which
draws them.*

—RALPH WALDO EMERSON

Anyone who can still remember the days before children will remember how well-ordered the house seemed to be. Even if your house was not something from a magazine, today's memory of it rivals anything Martha Stewart could put together. You knew back then that if you walked downstairs in the dark of night you would not step on anything that squeaked or talked. If friends were to come over for dinner, you knew exactly what the evening would entail. You cooked the dinner and everyone ate it, no big surprises. You knew that if you turned on the TV to watch a game, most likely you could still be watching it when the game ended. Friends, you remember, were not afraid to call, visit, or invite you over. Now you sense they are wondering how to handle your "situation." Here are a few tips I have for friends who want to visit. You might find a familiar ring to them.

1. Dinnertime is definitely not the time to call us. The only way it is safe to talk to us at that time is if you are actually with us in person. Otherwise expect a lot of noise and more shushing than real conversation. Sometimes we forget the question you ask thirty seconds after you asked it. It's not that it wasn't a worthwhile question, it is just that one of the kids just forced a french fry into a place where it doesn't belong.

2. Don't ring the doorbell if you visit mid-afternoon. It is likely you will wake someone. If the kids are asleep, every minute is sacred. Knock.

3. If you come for dinner, figure out a way to let us know (without our having to ask—that feels impolite) if you are going to stay past the kids' bedtime. Will you be gone when we get back downstairs after putting the kids to bed? We want you to stay, but we don't want to be presumptuous. (OK, I'll be honest. We are afraid you will sneak out when we turn our backs on you, thus the deadbolts on every door. We are just desperate for adult company.) Know that you are welcome to linger as long as you want. If you are staying, feel free to join in on the bedtime routine if you'd like. Read a book, give a bath, do whatever you want. The kids love it, and we will welcome the post-bedtime comfort of being with friends.

4. When you come to visit, make yourself at home.

5. Don't feel like you have to be with the kids all the time. They can play by themselves, and they have to learn that adults need time to talk, and that they are not always the center of attention.

6. We have become somewhat accustomed to our chaotic surroundings, so we apologize for the mess. Don't judge our circumstances by the clutter—it is much better (and sometimes much worse) than it looks. Don't feel you have to clean, unless that makes you feel at home.

7. Yes, you may correct our children when they are acting up. If you weren't a friend, you wouldn't be visiting. Our kids are expected to learn how to respect adults, and they are expected to listen to our friends. It takes a village, so they say. Just be gentle.

8. If you invite us to your house for dinner, please let us know up-front if the kids are invited, and (this is important) it is perfectly OK if they are not. Also, we hate to sound picky, but if they are invited, please try to have some kid-friendly food to accompany the blackened trout and asparagus spears.

9. You do not need to give the children gifts. If you choose to do so, keep it simple. Sometimes things break within twenty-four hours of being unwrapped. Don't be insulted. Recognize that the gift was loved to its early demise.

10. Try to ignore the fact that four children are spinning around the room, unless you feel impelled to join them. Try to act natural when the decibel level reaches illegal heights. Close your eyes, breathe deeply, and imagine you are on your own sofa at home. We

will cover the dry cleaning expenses when grape juice is poured on your sweater.

11. Stop by when you are in the neighborhood. It is a big deal for us to make plans, so feel free to be spontaneous. We are almost always home. (Just watch yourself as you walk around the family room. Don't trip over anything. I don't think we carry enough insurance.)

12. There is no such thing as too early, but there is such a thing as too late. If you happen to be delivering the morning paper, that is a great time to visit. If you are driving home after the 9:30 p.m. movie lets out, visiting hours are, unfortunately, over.

Opening our house to friends has always been important to Felicia and me. Although children have certainly complicated things, our desire for hospitality remains. Now we just need to be more creative, more resilient, and more reliant on our friends' good nature. This stage will end, and soon we will cook dinner for friends once again without the risk of a stuffed animal clogging the toilet and flooding the house before the second course. We hope our friends are patient with us until that day comes. More important, we hope our friends can join us in the chaos until then.

God of open arms,
make our home a welcoming place;
a warm place that invites, renews,
refreshes, and delights.
May our door be always open
to friend and stranger alike.

CHAPTER 14

Icy Morning Fantasy

Have courage for the great sorrows of life
and patience for the small ones;
and when you have laboriously accomplished
your daily task, go to sleep in peace.
God is awake.

—VICTOR HUGO

The other night my wife and I sat at a table that was not our own, were asked what we would like to eat and drink, and then were served that which we requested. There was nobody to feed. They didn't even have any plastic plates or baby spoons. The other people in attendance were not related to us, nor were they eating the same food we were eating. Not once did I have to ask anyone if they washed their hands. We were in a place that I used to be familiar with but have not been inside in a long while. It is called a restaurant.

Dinner out is a rare occasion for us now; it sits on the shelf alongside the many other evening activities that we formerly enjoyed. We often comment that the last time we were inside a movie theater was when Felicia was pregnant with our first-born. Every other movie we have seen since then has been from the comfort of our own couch.

If we venture out, we do so after the baby is asleep. We feel that we cannot knowingly put another person through that which we endure every night with four bed-time routines. Often our night out is simply playing cards with friends. The adult conversations, adult laughter, and adult political arguments are all welcomed diversions from the everyday.

My mother seems to have made it across the vast, dangerous crevasse of raising kids, and is thriving on the other side. One morning revealed just how different her stage of parenting is from mine. The February roads were covered in ice, so nobody left the house; a phone call to my mother (enjoying her winter in Florida) put things in perspective.

My mother joked, "Oh, so you are stuck inside today? So that means you are curling up with a good book."

"Very funny, Mom," I said, "I haven't done that in five years." My mother assured me that the time will come again, faster than I know it.

Most people with grown children will tell me that. This time is fleeting, they say; the days will rush by and soon enough the children will be grown. While that is hard to believe, something inside me tells me to try to believe it. Try to look at today as a gift.

I love the concept of being able to go to a restaurant or call friends for a quiet evening without preparing four days in advance in order to secure a babysitter. I love the idea of reading a book on an icy morning—a book that doesn't involve a cat with a red-striped hat on his head. But that day is certainly not today.

The goal of the day is often just making it to the night, but my prayer rises up against that. My prayer is instead to be able to love the day. Bedtime's quiet should be an opportunity to celebrate the day's wonder. Most often, however, bedtime is simply an experience of relief that the children are finally silent.

The life of a parent of very small children is one of physical exhaustion. I have noted that the life of a parent of older children is often one of emotional exhaustion. In contrast (and my mother's phone call supports this), I imagine that the life of a parent of grown children—children who are off on their own with their own families—is a life of peace and simplicity, with the continual, delightful prospect of wild nights of fun and frolic.

I know the reality will be different from the fantasy, since reality is always much different from the imagined, but I can still take pleasure in the fantasy. Carrying two children down the basement steps to prepare watercolors for the icy morning's activities requires some fantasy. It requires a moment's belief that someday it will be easy again.

For now, however, I live in the moment. Dinner is ready. Did everyone wash their hands? Where's that baby spoon?

God of understanding,
it is sometimes hard to be here,
hard to be at another's service
every hour of every day.
I long for rest, I long for privacy,
and I long for time.
Grant me the ability to see the beauty
even in the difficult times,
to appreciate the moment and celebrate this life
rather than just endure it.

CHAPTER 15

Whose Words Are They, Anyway?

*By the time a man realizes
that maybe his father was right,
he usually has a son who thinks he is wrong.*

—CHARLES WADSWORTH

It finally happened. I finally answered the question, "Why not?" with "Because I am the daddy and I said 'No.'" My four-year-old son, of course, responded with the completely logical, "Well I am the boy and I say, 'Yes.'" Two persons of equal dignity and value before God, but who possess entirely different viewpoints on their positions of authority in the home.

I have tried hard not to use the position of strength that my size and age grant me by default. I have tried not to wave the banner of "I am bigger, and therefore right" in our family's parade as we march onward. But sometimes it is a statement that is next to impossible to avoid. Sometimes the only real answer is, indeed, "Because I said so." Every other answer is just too exhausting to explain.

The children think that the answer changes with time. They think that if a question is asked seventeen times, then the eighteenth attempt will grant them access. They think that crying and stomping and whining changes my heart so that it is easier for me to assent. Oh, how much they have to learn. Of course, I am sure they would say the same thing about me.

It sounds cliché to mention that I hear my parents in my own responses to my children, but it is true. I have a feeling that no one really disciplines their own children, but they actually just let the words of the previous generation do the work for them. My children have been told that those lima beans are actually very good; they should just try them. Somehow I know that I am not telling my children that; rather, my mother tells them to eat their vegetables through me.

If they can't play nicely with that truck, then they won't play at all. I think my sister and I had the exact same truck come between us, and our mother used the exact same reasoning. In the midst of Clare's tears, she hears me say, "Are you laughing or are you crying?" She hears my voice, but my father's words. I am certain that I did not really say, "If I hear that again, I am stopping this car right now," but my children were witnesses, and they will tell you that I was indeed the one behind the wheel.

Our parents are actually the driving forces behind our ongoing, relentless pursuit of forming children who might behave well in the real world. Felicia and I were lucky to have been raised with loving discipline, but even so, we have had to adjust some of our parents' techniques to suit the times. We have left out the tactics that we just cannot agree with, but essentially the message is the same: You will poke your eye out, and your face will freeze that way. Today, the now-grandparents can just stand there and think the kids are cute. They think that we are the ones who are in charge of discipline, and that they are the ones in charge of playing. Oh, how much they have to learn.

We are well aware that strong childhood influences rule our thinking. Thank God our particular childhood influences are not doing damage, and that, for the most part, we concur with our parents' beliefs about raising kids. I, however, am confident that I will never say, "Stop that crying or I'll give you something to cry about." Wait a minute. There was a point when I was convinced I would never attempt the brilliant argument of "Because I am the daddy," either.

Never is a very long time. I think parenthood has a tendency to turn "never" into "not until I have absolutely no other way of reasoning my way out of this one." I am sure many of my parents' "nevers" became some of my very own childhood memories. I bet my mother once said she would never wipe her children's faces with her own saliva. Look where that "never" got us. Come to think of it, look where that "never" got my own kids.

God of our tradition,

our stories, legends, myths, and prayers

are handed down from parent to child.

So, too, our character.

Help me to rely on the lessons

I learned from my parents.

Help me to give the very best of our tradition

to my children.

CHAPTER 16

Let Me Count the Ways

The lesson which life repeats
and constantly enforces
is "look under foot."
You are always nearer the divine
and the true sources of your power than you think.

—JOHN BURROUGHS

"Do you know how much I love you? More than all the snow on the ground. . . . More than all the trees in the neighborhood. . . . More than all the grass in the park. . . . More than five Christmases." My children and I play a game where we tell each other how much we love the other. The announcement always ends with the recipient of the love saying, "Thanks, that's a lot of love." I usually end the game when someone mentions "more than the whole world and the sun and all the planets." It is just hard to top that one without trying to explain "universe" to a three-year-old. I am

reminded of an essay question that one of my students once suggested I include on a test: "Define 'universe.' Give two examples."

This is just a game we play, but sometimes, depending on the day and the circumstances, it doesn't feel like a game. It feels like something more, like we have actually scratched the eternal and discovered that we have always been together. There is a line in scripture that says "Before I formed you in the womb, I knew you." That line, I am coming to realize, does not only describe the relationship God has to creation, but also the relationship parents have to their children. We somehow have always been together.

I had no idea what to expect when the first child was born. I could not have known just how connected I would be to these children, how much a part of me they truly would be. It took night after night of bedtime stories and cuddling to show me. It took Band-Aid after Band-Aid to offer me the chance to know how connected we are. It took the children's own astonishing revelations to show me: a casual comment about the meteor that put an end to the dinosaurs (complete with the use of the word "extinct"), a child's memory of a summer trip that happened one-third of a lifetime ago, a toddler running up to me with the word "Daddy," and even the tears of a two-year-old telling me to stop laughing at him when I smiled about something cute he had just said. The depth of love's mystery is found in these children. In the midst of this mystery, the "I love you more than . . ." game takes on a new meaning. It certainly is more than a game.

Love is not always easy or obvious. Clearly love is not the first word I would use to describe the experience of telling Paddy for the sixth time to put on his pajamas. When Clare changes her mind about what she wants to wear so often that I run out of the house screaming, love's mystery is truly hidden. When Liam has climbed onto the kitchen table after being removed from the very same table three times, love's mystery is illusive. When all four children have tag-teamed a sleepless night for Felicia and me, love is something that appears to have been lost, along with that doll's shoe that we just can't seem to find anymore.

At times like these, I have to rely on the faith that tells me that the love will be obvious once again. I have to deliberately remember that after Clare's furor over my bad choice in tights ("No! Not those! The BLUE ones!"), she will indeed smile, climb on my lap, and tell me her plans for a wonderful birthday party. When Jack won't allow me to take him out of the crib in the morning because Mommy is supposed to do it, I have to remember that he will be the first to greet me that night when I come home from work. The love remains, but it is not always floating on the surface. Many times I only encounter it when I hold my breath and dive down to the bottom. The challenge is to keep diving.

Certainly life with four small children is not always easy. Still, it is also not the disaster that deserves the frightened, deer-in-the-headlights stares from strangers when they hear that our four children were all born within four years. Four small children offer a series of moments that come together to make up a life. Like anyone's life, the moments vary in intensity, and often the love lies hidden, waiting for a chance to reveal itself once again to an unsuspecting dad. That love is bigger than the backyard, higher than the Ferris wheel, and deeper than Winnie the Pooh's appetite. That love is as mysterious as the universe.

Funny, I think I can, indeed, give more than one example for universe. I think I can give four.

God whose love is eternal,

let me see your love

in the faces and lives of my children.

Help me to know such love

in both the good times and the hard times.

CHAPTER 17

Potluck Living

If I could persuade myself that I should find [God]
in a Himalayan cave,
I would proceed there immediately.
But I know that I cannot find [God]
apart from humanity.

—MOHANDAS K. GANDHI

Easter in the final week of Felicia's first pregnancy was a spectacular feast. We had planned it for a long time and cooked for days. We had friends over for dinner, and we shared several courses of food, each accompanied by a different wine. Seated around the dining room table, we ate off the good china and drank from crystal goblets. My grandmother's Irish linen was cleaned and pressed for the occasion. Flowers were on the table and music played softly in the background. Dinner took at least two hours. Afterward we had an Easter egg hunt, just for laughs.

This past Easter could not have been more different. Two families came to the house for dinner. The total child count was nine, and the oldest was six. The wine was opened but not poured. Anyone who could find a plastic cup was welcome to it. Everyone brought something to eat and drink, so I took a ham out of the oven and put it on the counter. Everyone else threw their donations on the counter as well, and the paper plates were passed around. The children sat at various tables in the kitchen as their parents hovered over them, helping them eat. Laughter and conversation drowned out *The Little Mermaid* tape in the stereo. Adults eventually ate their food while standing, after having warmed up their full paper plates in the microwave. Eating took about sixteen minutes. The Easter egg hunt took hours.

What a contrast, but what a delight. Both meals celebrated friends and family, both honored the transforming power of God, both celebrated Easter's message of new life. But neither could be recognized as even resembling the other. The earlier Easter boasted special foods, special breads, and special clothes. The latter Easter boasted special people. The first was truly an exceptional celebration, a memorable evening. The last was a moment in time, a snapshot taken of life in this new stage, life among and for children. Both were wonderful events. They are, perhaps, each even more wonderful when understood in the contrast.

Formal meals have given way to potluck suppers, a metaphor for this life. Each of us brings what we have to the table, in whatever container we found it. The containers do not match each other, but they celebrate each other nonetheless. The refrigerator stands ready to be explored, and the wine, beer, and apple juice await the hand that reaches for them. Anyone who expects something to be poured into his or her glass might have to wait a while. This life requires action, movement. Those who stand still will miss something.

This potluck supper celebrates life as it is. We come as we are and experience whatever happens to be in store for us at the time. Little can be planned in advance. The basics are put in the oven and the rest is up to the company. The food is important, certainly, but the conversation and the play make the day unique. We celebrate the life hidden with every Easter egg, and the cameras are aimed at the future, not at the perfect centerpiece.

I hope our Easter meals are always potluck suppers. I hope our friends are always ready to celebrate with us, and I hope our children will always eagerly hunt for eggs. Life will probably never be a perfect five-course meal again, but I think in many ways it was never meant to be so for us. I think the multicolored eggs, the wide variety of casserole dishes, and the wine drunk from plastic cups have always been where we were heading. It just took a faith-filled leap into the messiness to find it.

God of new life,
our gathering is made sacred
by your very presence.
Help us to celebrate each other as we celebrate you;
just as we are, face to face, hand to hand.

CHAPTER 18

Someone Who Remembers

*A friend may well be reckoned
the masterpiece of nature.*

—RALPH WALDO EMERSON

I have known Pat since I was twenty years old. There has not been a time in the many years since we met when we were not in contact with each other. Though a good portion of those years was spent living a distance from each other, we managed to remain in touch and we kept each other updated on the details of our lives. Two years ago we ended up in the same place once again. I moved into the town where she has lived for a good many years. This time, however, I didn't come alone.

There is something special about being with some-one who knew me in my youth. Pat brings a thread of stability, wisdom, and peacefulness, and she encourages me to keep stretching, to keep seeking the things that I wanted when I was young. She reminds me of my earliest promises to myself and to the world. And she reminds me of the life I wanted to be living down the road; the life that, coincidentally, I am truly living now.

She takes the long view when she watches me parent my children. She remembers when their dad was just a kid himself, so she has a unique perspective on the relationship. I never would have dreamed during my days of trying to find a clean shirt in my dorm room that Pat would be present when our fourth child was born at home. But she was there, and she even videotaped it, something that even I wouldn't have agreed to do before I had children myself.

I don't think I have actually ever voiced this to the kids, but they have figured out for themselves that Pat is family. When saying prayers at night, they ask for a blessing over her, along with Grandma and Uncle Jay and the rest. When drawing or painting, her blank refrigerator door is often the subject of the children's concern, so she ends up with many brilliant works of art. We expect to celebrate birthdays in her company, and when making plans for a sledding trip or a bike ride, her name comes up.

It is a blessing to be back with Pat. Everyone should spend their adulthood with at least one person who knew them in their youth. It keeps us honest, it keeps us faithful, and it keeps us connected to our dreams.

God who gathers us,
I thank you for my friendships,
especially for those who have known me the longest.
Keep the friendships strong.
May I always celebrate these friends
as the circle grows stronger and wider
with every day.

CHAPTER 19

I Was Mistaken

*I hear and I forget. I see and I remember.
I do and I understand.*

—CONFUCIUS

One of the things that I have wanted to do since the children were born is to seek forgiveness from many different people whom I encountered during my childless days. These are people who would most likely not remember me, nor would they necessarily know my name. They are the anonymous parents upon whom I passed judgment.

They are the parents of children I saw at church, the parents who, sweating and exhausted, tried to silence exuberant voices. They are the parents I saw in a restaurant with a crying baby—out much too late with that child, in my opinion. They are the parents of children who ran around the grocery store, the parents of children unleashed onto a playground. Though I would never have admitted it to myself then, I found out after having my own children that I had been unfair. And I am paying for it now.

Every time my child comes downstairs with "one more thing to say" before he finally stays in bed for the night, I pay for my earlier thoughts about parents who were not disciplined enough with their child's bedtime. Every time I offer another piece of buttered bread to a child who won't eat her carrots, just to be sure she eats *something*, I pay for my earlier question about why some children can be so fussy with their food. Every time I stop my phone conversation to address a child's relentless questioning, I pay for the times I rolled my eyes while talking to someone who allowed his child to interrupt an adult conversation.

Before, my only model was a long-ago memory— faded and romanticized with time—of my own perfect behavior as a child. I would *never* have done that, I was certain. My parents would *never* have let me behave that way. Well, four children later, and a grandmother who is perfectly willing to remind me of how misbehaved I actually was, I have learned my lesson.

Any parent brave enough to bring his or her children to church should be commended, no matter how difficult it is to hear the sermon. Any parent who is able to shop for groceries and leave the store without a bleeding child should be praised. Any parent who is able to provide a meal for the children, bring them to the park, and get them safely to bed at night should be honored. If that parent happens to be able to talk on the phone when the children are awake, every half-sentence that is uttered is gold.

I regret the illusion of wisdom that I once lived with. I had no idea whatsoever. I now think back with a certain amount of envy to that person who had his baby in the restaurant at 9:30 p.m. I am now proud of him for doing it. I now know that the little girl who I once saw wearing a frighteningly bright yellow shirt that covered a red plaid wool dress was exceedingly happy that her mother let her choose her own outfit that day. Or her mother was just happy that the clothes argument ended and she was able to get out of the house. I now know that yes, indeed, candy needs to be put out of reach and not on the coffee table. Children will not be able to just say no. It does not mean they are an undisciplined, unruly bunch. It means that they are children.

So I apologize to the parents of the child at the beach who ate sand, the parents of the one who took another's bucket, and the parents of the one who cried when it was time to leave. I apologize to the parents of the boys with uncombed hair, the girls with chocolate on their faces, and the babies whose diapers needed to be changed. I assure you I am now paying dearly for the unspoken thoughts I harbored. In fact, I now thank you for paving the way, because I am sure that somewhere in the collective unconscious of parenthood, you prepared me in some small way for my present existence. You are to be commended, one and all.

God of mercy,
forgive me the times
when I failed to see another's goodness,
when I judged based on my own limited knowledge,
when charity was not my first impulse.
Help me to always celebrate another's blessing,
rejoice in another's striving,
and assist in another's struggle.

CHAPTER 20

A Crown for Each

Everything, by an impulse of its own nature,
tends towards its perfection.

—DANTE

We have a bit of an unusual custom in our house when it comes to birthdays. A birthday requires a crown. I am not quite sure where it began, but it is certainly elevated to the status of unchangeable law now. We must make a crown out of cereal boxes for each birthday girl or boy.

I am impressed by the child's need for ritual. While sometimes it gets in the way—since it would certainly be easier not to have to construct a crown each time—I am impressed by their desire for something to be the same, for something to comfort them and to give meaning and purpose to the day. The cake can be bought or made (though baking it is usually a part of the ritual), the candles can have numbers on them or not, the presents (at least at this stage) can be a part of it or not, but the crown is a requirement.

We measure the child's head and then tape the cardboard to fit. We cut the top of the crown to give it the telltale series of points. We glue construction paper to the crown, and then the fun begins. The children all join in on designing the crown with the birthday girl or boy's name on it, his or her age, and then drawings of things that that child most enjoys. The key is to get the colors right, since they each have their particular favorites, and it is an added bonus if there is glitter to include. The child then wears the crown when we sing "Happy Birthday," and usually continues to wear the crown while eating the cake.

Birthdays are talked about long in advance of the day itself. The older two are now in school, so they hope to have parties that include their friends. Paddy is learning how to write, so he writes a couple invitations each day and gives himself several months to complete the task. On each birthday, all the children are measured on the kitchen wall where we mark their heights, so before the big day, they all practice standing against that wall, putting their hands up on top of their heads, and quickly turning to see if they have grown at all since the last time they were measured.

Birthdays are celebrations of family. Each child participates in some way, so each child celebrates the other. "Happy Birthday" is one of the first songs that each of them learned, because, let's face it, there are a lot of birthdays in our house. The day is about honoring the person, and fortunately the gifts are still secondary to that. A time will come, I know, when the crowns will die out in popularity and the newest game or toy will take center stage. But for now, we can take delight in the ritual.

When Paddy turned three he announced as he went to bed that that was the best birthday in sixty-five million years. Perhaps that was true, but he doesn't remember the first one. I get to compare each subsequent birthday with the actual experience of the children's births. The crowns they wore on those days were not made of cereal boxes, but they were crowns nonetheless, made of God's delight, and God's assurance that life would never be the same.

God of every embrace,
let me know your beauty in my children,
in their ritual and their spontaneity,
in their delight, their frustration,
and their wonder.
Be the source and the focus
of our customs and celebrations.
Be the wonder of the moment.

CHAPTER 21

Peace on the Pillows

The lights begin to twinkle from the rocks;
The long day wanes; the slow moon climbs; the deep
Moans round with many voices. Come, my friends.
'Tis not too late to seek a newer world.

—ALFRED, LORD TENNYSON

Someone once gave my wife a helpful tip early in our parenting. She told Felicia to look in on the children when they are sleeping. Perhaps that does not seem so profound or extraordinary, but I assure you that there is a great deal of wisdom in that little piece of advice. I have gotten to the point where it is a nightly routine for me. I now find that I must look in or my day is not finished. If I don't see my children asleep, I have missed an opportunity for hope, I have passed up a chance at peace.

When they are sleeping, they are—excuse the expression—perfect. When they are sleeping, they are not using permanent markers on the wallpaper. When they are sleeping, they are not yelling at each other. When they are sleeping, they do not talk back, they do not say the meal is yucky, they do not throw Jell-O. When they are sleeping, they are the clearest argument for why the world should keep going. They are peace personified. They are as they were created to be, just under the angels.

The goal is to remember them asleep. The goal is to remember their sleeping gentleness as I am trying to get out of the house in the morning, get them to school, and make it to the office somewhat near the start of the workday. If I can remember them asleep, then pulling them out of mud puddles is a little easier. Thinking of their beauty in the midst of their slumber, I can gather the patience to sing "Row, Row, Row Your Boat" yet another time. I need to see them sleep because I need to remember them that way. I need to remember what miracles they truly are.

Sometimes I think things in general would work more smoothly if we all could be seen sleeping, if each of us could be remembered as a miracle. If people who don't understand us could see us asleep, their attitude toward us might change. If the people I have difficulty with would just let me peek in one night, maybe I would be able to deal with them with a little more kindness. When we are sleeping, resting our tired bodies, gathering strength for the coming day, and experiencing dreams that keep us sane, we are, like the children, perfect.

I bet that's why we are all able to keep going. I bet it is because God has seen us sleep. And God remembers us asleep. God remembers, especially when we throw Jell-O or write on walls or play with someone else's blocks. When we are impatient and cruel and arrogant, God remembers, and forgives.

Of course, the next best thing to watching the children sleep is to walk into the bathroom late at night to see my daughter falling asleep on the potty, but that is another story altogether. Believe me, though, that is an easy image to remember, and it has helped me through many trying situations.

God who remembers,

your compassion is our life.

Let your mercy be our mercy,

so that we may treat our children as you treat us.

May we remember their perfection in difficult times,

and love them always.

CHAPTER 22

Tending the Garden

There is not a flower that opens, not a seed that
falls into the ground, and not an ear of wheat that
nods on the end of its stalk in the wind that does
not preach and proclaim the greatness and the
mercy of God to the world.

—THOMAS MERTON

Gardening is a way to connect myself to my early childhood. It brings me to a simpler time. When I am planting, trimming, or cleaning out flower beds, I am brought to a day long ago when I was sitting on the grass in the heat of the summer, watching my grandparents work in their garden.

Gardening lasts from the depths of winter when I start thinking about what I will do in the spring, to the end of autumn when it is time to plant the bulbs. There is always a promise of something more, always something to learn, always something new to explore. And best of all, my children are now involved.

We have sections of each garden that are designated child-only zones. That's where they can dig and plant to their hearts' content. I have long given up on stopping toddlers from walking through the beds, but at least the sections of the gardens that are just for them make me feel like I am somehow combating that. They can pick the seeds they want, or go with me to the nursery to find some plants. They have their own watering cans, and if they are extra careful they can even use the hose once in a while.

They love to get dirty, of course, but they also like the fact that their mother bought them their very own gardening gloves. It is usually a dilemma for them: to wear the gloves, or get dirt on their hands. It is not an easy choice.

When they take part in deciding what is to go into the garden, the decisions are based solely on color. Clare insists on pink flowers, and Paddy wants purple ones. Fortunately petunias come in both colors, so we have a bed filled with them. The children know how to snip off the spent blossom to allow the plant to thrive, and they do that with a certain glee. Of course, "snipping off" the blossom often means pulling the entire plant from the root, but that is why we have so many plants in the first place.

A major task for them is to take the seed pods off the marigolds and save them in paper bags. They have become quite good at this, and they look forward to the time when the seeds they collected can be planted. Each of us has a different style. I take the whole clump and drop it in the bag. Paddy opens up the clump of seeds and drops them individually, very carefully, into the bag. Clare removes bright flowers, fully in bloom, and tries to convince me that they are dried up and only the seeds are left. Jack simply picks the flowers for his mom and dad. He is absolutely not interested in saving anything for the next season. Liam just tries to eat whatever he can get his hands on: seeds, blossom, leaf, or dirt.

The compost bin in the backyard is also a source of excitement. The kids are in charge of carrying the kitchen scraps out to drop in it. They know how to make a little hole for the scraps, and then how to cover them up. They know that the compost needs dried leaves and grass to work. They know that it should be moist, like a sponge. They know about the heat that the compost creates, and have amazed more than one person by telling them about the microbes at work. Paddy will tell you the life of the compost heap any time he gets the opportunity: "It all starts with garbage," he always begins. Then he talks about the microbes eating everything and concludes with the same words every time: "And then you have beautiful compost; it's like black soil, perfect for feeding your vegetables and flowers." I think he heard about it in a book, because I certainly had not used the word "microbes" when explaining composting to him.

The garden is a great place to be with children. It teaches them about the benefits of work and the mystery of life and growth. They appreciate the beauty of the flowers, and they enjoy looking at all the different types of leaves and blossoms. They love to touch the earth and to carefully prepare a place for their own seeds. Most of all, I think, they love to be outside with their mom and dad. Just like I did when I was a kid.

I realize that half of what I know about gardening comes from what I learned when I was not much older than my own children are now. My grandparents taught me by simply letting me watch, and sometimes by letting me do the work. Those lessons have remained with me all these years. I am sure my grandfather did not buy a marigold seed in forty years. He simply removed the seeds from the plants themselves. With the help of these little hands, I intend never to have to buy another marigold seed myself. More important, with the help of these little hands, I intend to be constantly amazed that those tiny seeds can actually grow into beautiful plants, and that life's longing for itself demands that the plants in turn make more seeds. That is the wonder of gardening. A wonder that adults sometimes forget, but that children never will.

God of all creation,
bring us to your garden.
Be with us as we share our time in your wonder,
help us to always stand in awe of your mystery.
May we always share in your goodness together.

CHAPTER 23

"Up in the Air—Is It a Bird? A Plane?"

Grief can take care of itself,
but to get the full value of a joy
you must have someone to divide it with.

—MARK TWAIN

One of the great things about observing kids is to see how well they can play together. Clare and Jack make an interesting pair. None of the children antagonize each other so much as those two, but at the same time none of them play so well together either. Clare will snuggle on the couch with Jack and "read" to him. That same couch, however, can be the flash point of many arguments when Jack has invaded her space. She will dress up with him, sharing scarves and necklaces. But at other times when he puts on one of her hats, one would think that the walls are coming down. They are the best of friends and the worst of enemies, sometimes all within a two-hour stretch.

One Saturday morning I was impressed by how well they were playing. They were upstairs in Clare's bedroom, pretending to be at school. Occasionally they would come downstairs looking for a prop or two, announce once again what they were playing, and then head back upstairs to resume their game. I should know by now that such peaceful, silent play is often interrupted by that which is anything but silent and peaceful, but that day I had lulled myself into a state of blissful ignorance.

The crying that began to emanate from upstairs did not disturb me at first, but when it would not ease up, and it became more of a scream, I went to see what had happened. I found Clare slinking out of Jack's room, eyes wide, explaining, "I didn't do it." Never a good sign.

Jack was in the room, holding on to the side of the crib, crying his eyes out. It wasn't instantly obvious what had happened, but soon enough I realized what was going on. He was stuck. He had tried to climb over the side of the crib to get inside it, and instead had wedged his knee between the slats. Now he was suspended, not able to touch the floor, holding on by two little hands and one stuck knee.

My first reaction was that this was really not that big of a deal. If his knee could get in, then certainly it could come out. My attempts to release him from his state, however, were not successful. His knee absolutely would not come back the way it went in. His tears and his screaming just elevated my nervousness, which was quickly becoming a panic. I tried to pull the slats to see if they gave at all, but they were not to be budged. I tried forcing the knee back, only to be met with more agonizing screams. I looked to the part of the leg that was now hanging below the knee and wondered what was wrong. It looked distorted. Had the kneecap come loose? Was there a broken bone? Was there a dislocation? I couldn't tell how much of the crying was from fear and how much was from pain. My own panic only made it worse as I yelled at Clare to leave when she returned to see how her brother was doing. I didn't want her to be frightened by this sight, but my own fear was obvious. My son was hurt in my arms, but there was absolutely nothing I could do about it. I started to think about what would be best: to just break the slats with my hands, go and get a hacksaw, or call 911 and let the EMTs do it. He would need to be treated anyway. The way his leg was hanging, I was now certain that he had done serious damage.

Just as I was about to make up my mind about the next step, Felicia walked into the room. "He is stuck," I said in a shaky voice.

I thought she would be the one to call 911 while I stayed with Jack, or maybe she would get the hacksaw. Instead she said to me, "His foot needs to go through the slat, then you can take his whole leg out."

Felicia walked over to Jack, quietly said something soothing into his ear, pushed his foot through the slats of the crib, and gently pulled his leg out.

The crying stopped immediately. Only the after-puffs from a good long cry remained. He was not hurt; there was nothing loose, broken, or dislocated. There was just a little boy who had been scared because he had gotten himself stuck (and it wasn't the first time, obviously), and a daddy standing in the doorway taking his own pulse.

Clare wondered when this would all be over because she wanted to continue the game, Felicia brushed Jack off and headed back downstairs, and I called "Time and Temperature" to see if I were really still living on the same plane as everyone else. Minutes before, I had thought a trip to the ER was in store for us, along with a broken crib. Now I was watching my children return to their game of school and my wife return to reading to Paddy.

Some things are only funny well after they take place. This was one of those things. I could not believe that Felicia was so calm, and that the problem was so solvable. I couldn't believe I had panicked like I did, and that I couldn't figure out the obvious way to free him. Mostly, I couldn't believe just how different an experience it is to be someone who leaves the house for eight hours every day and someone who stays home. There are just some things that I will not have enough experience with. A child stuck in a crib, apparently, is one of them.

I found myself wondering what else happens during the day that I don't know about. What other life-threatening predicaments does Felicia save our children from on a daily basis? I pictured her with a cape, flying onto the scene to untie the kids from a train track as a locomotive comes barreling at them. Actually, knowing the way Clare and Jack play together—first as pals and then as sworn enemies—I think the likelihood of someone needing to be saved from a train disaster is not so far-fetched.

The seed of the superhero was planted when Felicia first said to me, "I think I am in labor," and it grew in strength as the family grew. Now that the children outnumber us, even Superman would be nervous around her. He may be a lot of things, but I am sure he is not faster than a falling baby or more powerful than a charging toddler. I bet he hasn't freed himself and others from nearly as many life-threatening scrapes as Felicia has.

Besides, she is only five years into her life as a superhero. I can only imagine what it will be like when all four kids are teenagers.

God of our salvation,
help me to know and appreciate
the work of my spouse,
help me to honor her patience and her insights.
May we continually learn from each other
and rely on each other's strength
in the raising of our children.

CHAPTER 24

Christmas Magic

We find a delight in the beauty and
happiness of children
that makes the heart too big for the body.

—RALPH WALDO EMERSON

We have no fireplace in our house, so Santa needs a key to get in. Fortunately, he mailed one to us this past Christmas, a nice big fancy key that he asked us to leave on the front porch for him. This way we don't have to leave the door unlocked. It worked wonders. Because there is no mantle for hanging the stockings, Santa brings them up to the children's rooms and places them on their beds. He also hangs a lighted wreath in each room, a colorful reminder of his visit. When the children wake up on Christmas morning, they spend a long time opening their stockings on their beds, talking about the mysterious visitor.

At the risk of having my children read this too early in life, I will admit that I am the one who hangs the wreaths and places the stockings. This is all a part of the fun of being a dad, experiencing the magic once again.

This past Christmas I decided to take it one step further. I borrowed a Santa suit from a friend, and in the middle of the night donned the outfit to bring the stockings to the rooms. All I wanted was for the kids to stir a little. I certainly did not want them wide awake, but I thought a nice, semi-dreamy state would be wonderful. I wanted just one eye to peek open. I thought it would be exciting, a magical experience for them.

I walked in, hung the wreaths, and then placed the stockings. Not a movement from the beds. I kicked the chair. Nothing. I Ho-Ho-Ho'ed. Not a twitch. I banged against the beds. Nothing but rhythmic breathing. Finally I Ho-Ho-Ho'ed and kicked the bed at the same time. And it happened. I saw Clare move her head and look at me. Felicia was outside the room (she couldn't be inside the room, because even Mommy shouldn't be awake when Santa comes) and I smiled at her, pointing to Clare's bed. By now Clare's head was back on the pillow, her eyes were closed, and she was breathing deeply. I couldn't tell if she had actually been awakened or not. So of course I kicked the bed again.

She moved her head a second time, this time not taking it off the pillow, but just peeking through one half-opened eye. Then the eye closed and she was back to deep breathing.

I left the room feeling a bit uncertain. I thought maybe she had seen me, but I could not be sure. I would ask in the morning.

The next day the kids woke us and we had a wonderful time in their bedrooms looking through the stockings and talking about Santa. They had, of course, left him some cookies and carrots for the reindeer. They wondered if the reindeer appreciated the snacks. We didn't have enough carrots so one of them got a celery stick, and we surmised that it must have been Dasher, because we thought he would like celery more than carrots. The children had sprinkled some magic dust on the snow in the front yard the evening before that was meant to attract the reindeer by both smell (it was oatmeal) and sight (it contained sprinkles that would light up in the moonlight). We wondered if that had worked. Finally I asked the question. Had anyone seen Santa last night?

The answer was no. No one had seen him, and I was disappointed. The conversation continued, but I admit that some of the magic was taken away from Daddy's Christmas. I was looking forward to talking about seeing Santa. At least we still had the presents downstairs, the note that Santa had left for the kids, the crumbs from the well-enjoyed cookies, and visits to friends' houses to look forward to. We had gone to church the night before, so this was to be a leisurely morning for us.

When we got downstairs, I encountered the magic that I thought I had missed in the bedroom. When Clare saw the presents, and saw that she had gotten the rocking chair (the pink one) that she had hoped for, she leaned over to me and whispered, "Daddy, I did see Santa last night. He came into our room, said 'Ho Ho Ho,' and pulled the blankets up to my chin."

The little sneak. She didn't want to reveal that she had seen the Big Man until she was assured that the presents would not disappear when she told her little secret. And more than that, she faked sleep. Our three-year-old was wise enough to fake sleep, complete with authentic-sounding deep breathing. I was amazed. I admit, I was also a bit impressed.

It is difficult to tell the children that a man named Santa visited in the night, it really is. It takes some getting used to. But I am able to do it because while I may be the one who places the stockings, Santa is still a part of the truth that is Christmas, and the children are eager to believe. They are eager to experience the wonder and the magic. I am convinced that a child who believes that a man in a red suit flies through the air behind reindeer can believe in a God who is closer to them than the air they breathe. If Santa can remember that we need a key mailed to us because we don't have a fireplace, then God can be born in an ancient village, entering into our lives as compassion itself. If Santa can know every child's name, then our children can believe that their every movement is embraced by love. The joy of experiencing such wonder, such faith, is profound.

The children know what we celebrate on Christmas. They know the facts through the words we tell them about our tradition, but they know the feelings through the mystery and the magic. They encounter Christmas through the stories, through the sights, through the smells, through the music, through all their senses. Just like they encounter love.

I don't think I will use a Santa suit in future years. I think I will let that memory stay just between Clare and Santa. I will let the magic remain a three-year-old's whisper. I will continue telling stories, though. I will tell stories about the reindeer and the elves, and I will tell stories about Bethlehem and the star. But I will not repeat the story you just read. In fact, this chapter will be ripped out of the copy we keep on our bookshelf. I don't want our kids to read it until the youngest is seventeen. I want Clare to believe in Santa until she goes to college.

And I want her to believe in love and a baby born in a stable for much longer than that.

God of all wonder,
thank you for my children's faith and joy.
Let their faith be my encouragement,
and their joy my hope.

CHAPTER 25

A Star's Challenge

A little child shall lead them.

—ISAIAH 11:6

I remember distinctly the day that Jack was born. He was born in a birth center that boasted a home-like atmosphere. No medical equipment (it was hidden, for use in emergencies only), no sounds of machines beeping, no pages over the P.A. system, no bright lights. He was born in a Victorian home on a queen-sized bed with a quilt that somebody's grandmother could have made. He was born peacefully, without the need for any medical interventions, just like his brothers and sister. He was born alert and smiling, ready to begin this new adventure. He had everything he needed from his mother, as he had had during the previous nine months. The world was ready for him, and he was ready for the world.

When we got home that night, I stood on the deck, looked up at the sky, and saw a shooting star. I understood why from the beginning people have looked to the heavens for signs. After a day like we had had, to see a star explode and dive into the night sky felt like a message from above. The message, I felt, was that this was a good day: a new person was born and the world was somehow a better place. There was a message of love, of endurance, of continuity. It was a message of hope.

Just before Jack was born, the country was mesmerized by reports of the death of a college student. This student had been beaten and strapped to a remote, abandoned fence post, left to die. He was beaten by people who didn't understand him, attacked because of their unwavering intolerance, killed because of their ignorance. He was murdered because he was not like them. He was dead because he was gay. And Jack was born in his wake. I think the hope-filled message of that shooting star was at the same time a challenge to remember that college student whenever I think of Jack's birth. I think it was a challenge to see Jack's birth as a possibility for something better, a reminder that life is not supposed to end on a fence post. Life is not supposed to end any more violently than it began.

Jack was born into a difficult world. He was born into a world suffering from intolerance. He was born into a world that says that some people are better than others, that the content of one's wallet determines one's worth, that one's sex, color, ethnicity, and sexual orientation define that person and give that person status. He was born into a world that has been fighting wars longer than anyone can remember, a world filled with people too poor to clothe their own children. He was born into a world that is broken. The shooting star, however, stands for possibility.

Becoming a dad meant taking on the world. I am responsible not only for my children but also for everyone's children who will someday encounter my own. I am responsible for the ones who will never meet my kids, but who will somehow be touched by their lives nonetheless. I am responsible for changing the way things are in whatever small way I can.

It sounds too dramatic perhaps, but it is true. Every opportunity for a child to experience love and community combats the message that says anything is OK as long as I get my way, that selfishness wins, and that greed is good. Every opportunity for a child to experience compassion makes the world a more compassionate place. Every opportunity for a child to experience peace makes the world a more peaceful place. When a child knows that her worth is based on who she is and not what she does, then others whom she encounters can experience such a sense of worth as well. The ends don't have to justify the means when the means are based in love. The ends will just flow naturally and logically from that love.

The earliest cultures recognized that the family is the basic unit of society, that for peace to rule the nation, peace must rule the family. The reflections in this book have been about simple things in the life of a new dad, the odd circumstances surrounding such a life, and the amusing and idiosyncratic elements of parenting. I hope in the long run, however, that the reflections are really about peace, about recognizing that in the midst of the chaos there is a possibility for order based on peace. Daddyhood is indeed an opportunity to have fun, to remember one's own childhood, to explore the possibilities found in marriage, to play and to run and to dive on the floor with abandon. Daddyhood is also an opportunity to change the world.

I hope that whatever my children turn out to be, rich or poor, married or unmarried, gay or straight, parents or not, that they will recognize and celebrate the dignity found in each person they encounter. I hope, too, that their country and their church will recognize their dignity as well. I hope that when they stand outside on the night a child is born—whether it happens to be their child or not—and see a shooting star, that that star will tell them that the world is indeed better because they are here. I hope that star tells them that the world has seen an end to people dying on fence posts, that the world has become a safe place where such a thing could not happen ever again.

I think that is what daddyhood is about: experiencing with a child the wonder of the world, the ups and downs of living with others, the joy-filled discovery of something new. I think daddyhood is simply about the future. It is about hope, a belief that these children will indeed make a difference. My heart points me to that, my faith reminds me of it, and that star that exploded and trailed across the horizon that night still pleads with me to make it so.

God of compassion,

remind me of your challenge to seek peace,

to fight indifference, and to change the world.

Help me in my obligation to raise my children

so that they may live and love in a world

that is made better by their very presence.

ABOUT THE AUTHOR

Daniel W. Driscoll, a father of four young children, wrote *Daddyhood* to "bring some meaning to the frequently chaotic life with kids." An editor with Ave Maria Press, Driscoll previously served as the director of parish social ministry for the Catholic diocese of Greensburg, Pennsylvania, and as a high school teacher in New Rochelle, New York. He has also worked as a hospital social worker.

A graduate of The Catholic University of America, Driscoll received a master of divinity from the University of Notre Dame. Driscoll authored a monthly column on peace and justice issues and has written numerous articles on marriage and family life. *Daddyhood* is his first book. He lives in South Bend, Indiana, with his wife, Felicia, and their children.